Cou…

on …

Body

CW01583294

Contents

Kurt Baze

RIGBY

You COUNT on your body every day!

You count on your bones to hold you up and your skin to hold you together.

You count on your muscles to move you and your nerves to tell you what hurts.

And many of the things you count on, you can count, too!

206 BONES

Did you know there are 206 bones in your body?

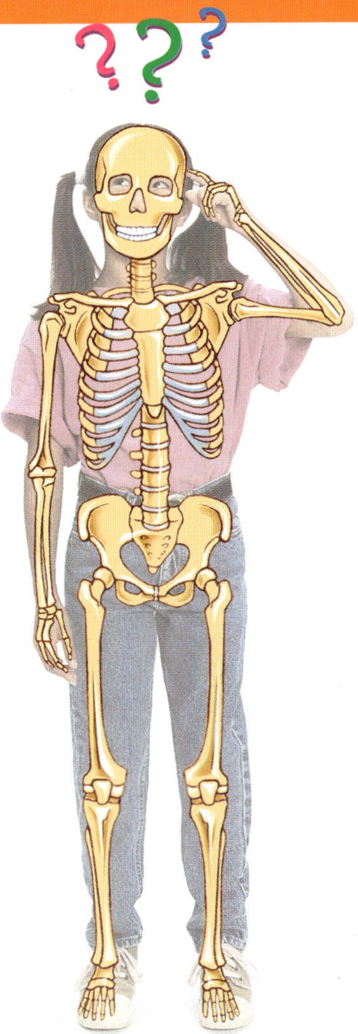

Can you guess how many bones are in your hands and feet?

a 20

b 44

c 106

You have 54 bones in your hands and wrists. You have 52 bones in your feet and ankles. That makes 106 bones – more than half of all the bones in your body!

660 MUSCLES

You have about 660 muscles in your body.

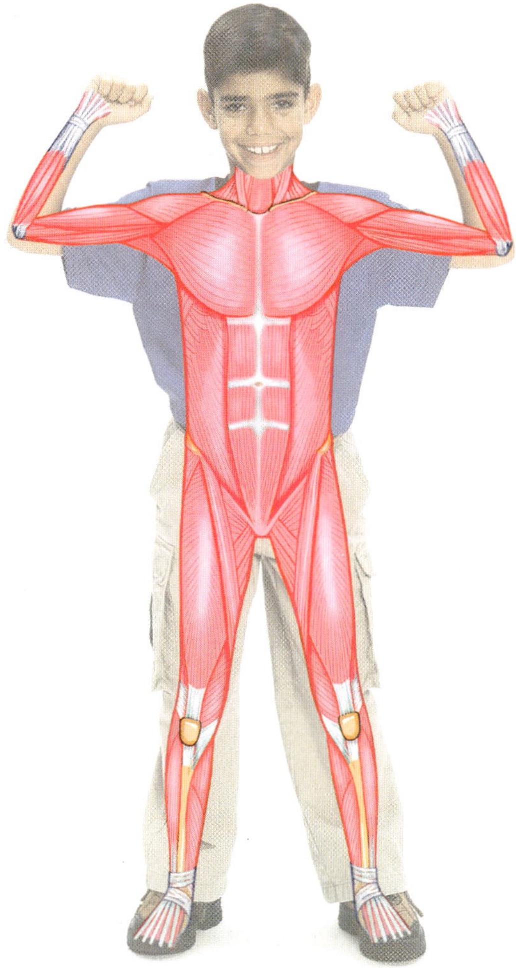

Can you guess how many muscles you use to take one step?

- (a) 200
- (b) 100
- (c) 10

You use 200 muscles to take a step! It doesn't matter whether it's a giant step or a tiny step.

▲ **A giant step and a tiny step use the same number of muscles.**

Did you Know?

Muscles make up about one half of your body weight. Your heart is a muscle – a very important one!

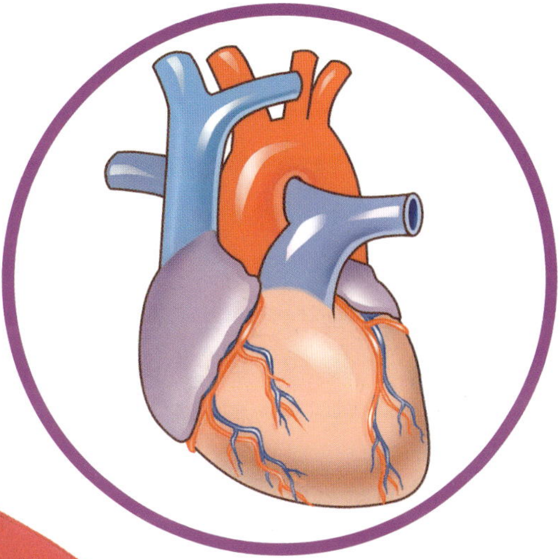

TRY THIS

Try to sit still for 30 seconds without moving a muscle.

How did you do?
Did you blink?
Did you breathe?
Did your heart beat?

Even when you sit very still, some muscles are moving. These are involuntary muscles – they move on their own. The muscles that move food down your throat and through your stomach, for example, are involuntary muscles.

2 000 000 SWEAT GLANDS

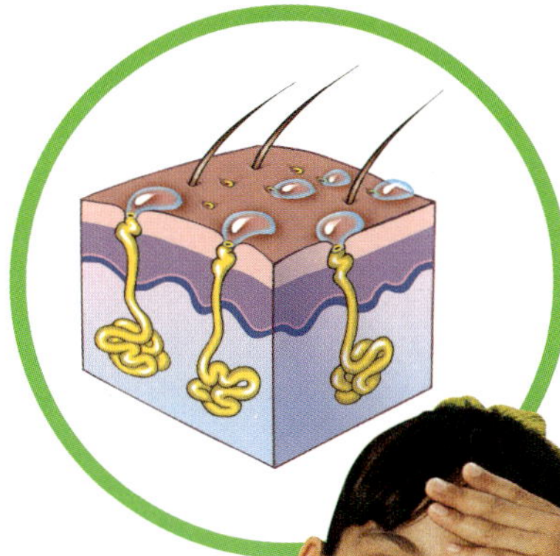

Sweat glands are tiny, coiled tubes in your skin. You have about 2 000 000 (two million) sweat glands in your skin.

Can you guess how tall each sweat gland would be if you uncoiled it?

- (a) as tall as an ant
- (b) as tall as a 10-year-old
- (c) as tall as a giraffe

Each sweat gland would be 122 centimetres tall!

100 000 HAIRS

You probably have more than 100 000 (one hundred thousand) hairs on your head.

Can you guess about how many hairs fall out each day?

a) 25 to 35

b) 70 to 100

c) 250 to 300

Each day, 70 to 100 hairs
fall out of your head!
It's a good thing they
grow back again!

Did you Know?

Hair grows faster on children than on adults. Also, hair grows faster in the summer than at other times of the year.

TRY THIS

Roll a straight hair and a curly hair between your thumb and finger.

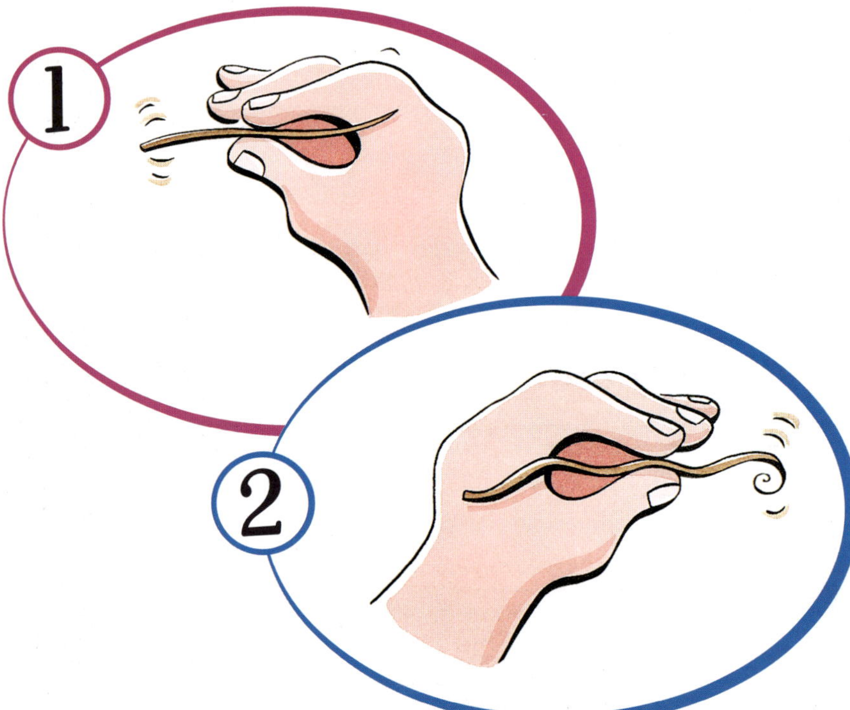

A straight hair is smooth and round, like a toothpick. A curly hair is also round, but it has flat places that make it feel rough when you roll it. Can you feel the difference?

1.3 KILOGRAMS OF BRAIN

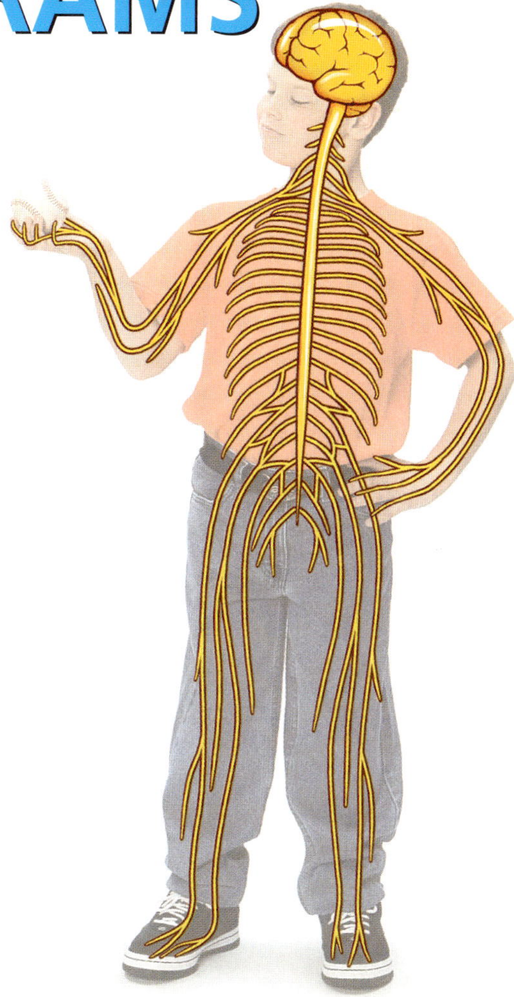

Your brain weighs about 1.3 kilograms. Information goes back and forth between your brain and the rest of your body every second. Nerves carry these messages.

Can you guess how fast nerve messages can travel?

- (a) as fast as a racing car
- (b) as fast as a bicycle
- (c) as fast as a jet plane

Nerve messages can travel up to 250 miles per hour along your nerve fibres.

2 LITRES OF BLOOD

Your body holds about 2 litres of blood. (Adults have about 5 litres of blood.) The blood travels through tubes in your body, called blood vessels.

Can you guess how far your blood vessels would reach if you connected them end to end?

a. twice around your school
b. twice around a football pitch
c. twice around the Earth

Your blood vessels would reach over 90 000 (ninety thousand) kilometres! That means they could circle the Earth more than two times.

Did you know?

Your heart beats 100 000 (one hundred thousand) times every day?

A blood cell makes the round trip between your heart and your knee in one minute.

TRY THIS

Open your hand wide, then squeeze it tight. Do this one time per second, for one whole minute.

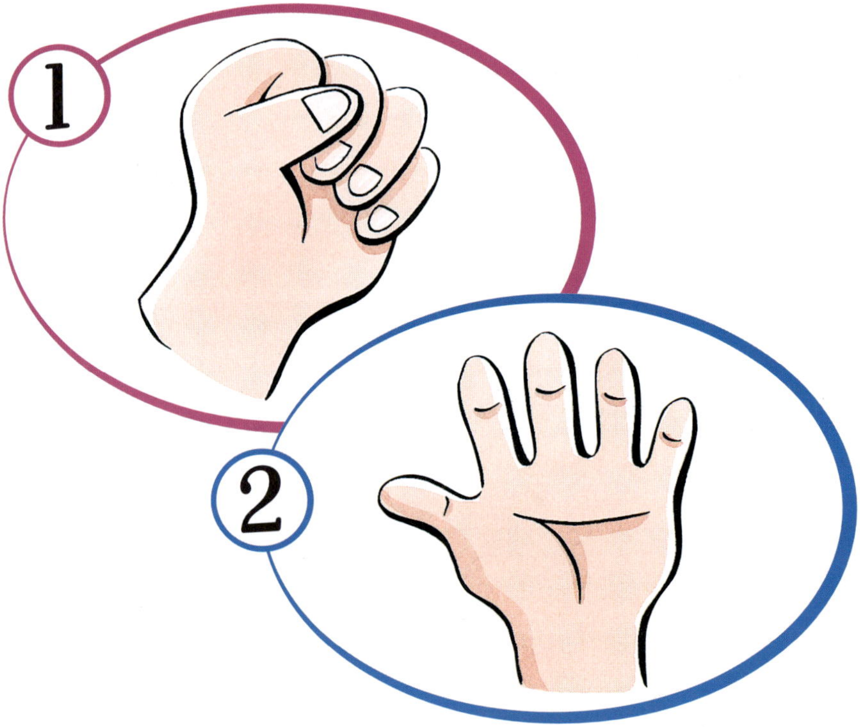

Was it hard to keep going? Your heart beats like this all the time – day and night – for your whole lifetime!

300 000 000 AIR SACS

You breathe air into and out of the 300 000 000 (three hundred million) air sacs in your lungs.

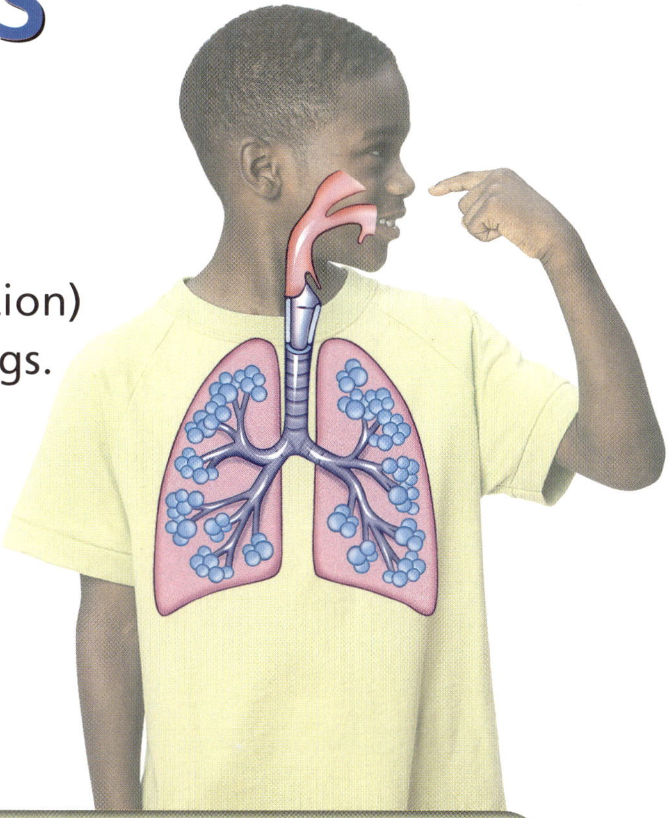

Can you guess how many litres of air you breathe out of your lungs every hour?

a 33 litres
b 330 litres
c 3 300 litres

Your lungs exhale about 330 litres of air each hour. That equals five and a half litres of air each minute.

At that rate, it would take you about five months to fill a hot-air balloon!

You COUNT on many parts of your body

See if you can guess how these numbers count in your body. Then turn the page to find out!

Then turn the page to find out!

a 1 000 000 000 000
b 2 500 000 000
c 15 000
d 2

a Your brain has about 1 000 000 000 000 (a million million) nerve cells.

b Your heart will beat about 2 500 000 000 (two thousand five hundred million) times in your lifetime.

c Your eyes blink about 15 000 (fifteen thousand) times each day.

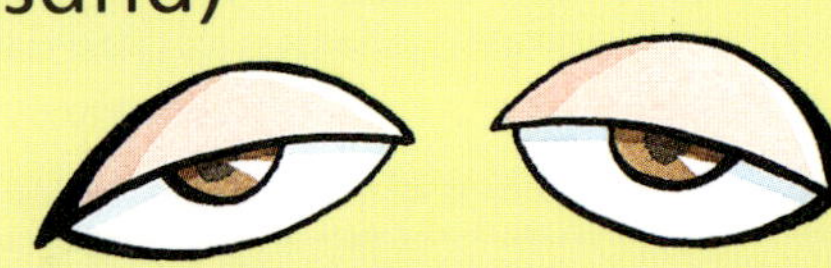

d Your body has lots of parts that come in twos. How many can you name?

Start counting!